"Never underestimate the power
you have to take your life
in a new direction"

-Germany Kent

By Certified Life Coach and Children's Author Reea Rodney

SELF-CELEBRATION WORKBOOK

Copyright © 2017 Dara Wisdom and Empowerment Coaching / Reea Rodney

All rights reserved. This book or any part of it, may not be reproduced, in any form without written permission.

Printed in the United States of America
ISBN: 978-0-9975059-8-6

Written by Reea Rodney
Illustrated by Alexandra Gold
Designed by FindlayCreative.com

If You Are Happy and You Know It Clap Your Hands
Improving Your Self-Celebration Workshop

Table of Contents

Page 4	Introduction
Page 5	About the Author
Page 6	What is Self-Celebration?
Page 7	Why is Self-Celebration Important?
Page 8	Why Celebrating your Failure is Important?
Page 9	Positive Impact of Self-Celebration
Page 10	Fun Ways to Promote Self-Celebration at Home or School
Page 11	Parents Tips for Promoting Self-Celebration

Self-Celebration Activities:

Page 12	Activity 1 – Introduce Yourself
Page 13	Activity 2 – It's All About Me
Page 14	Activity 3 – Celebrating Achievements
Page 15	Activity 4 – Things I Like About Myself
Page 16	Activity 5 - Facing Your Fears
Page 17	Activity 6 – Compliment Yourself
Page 18	Activity 7 – I Love Me Because...
Page 19	Activity 8 – I Am As...
Page 20	Activity 9 – Reward Certificate
Page 21	Activity 10 – Celebrating the Little Things
Page 22	Activity 11 – Celebrating a Hero
Page 23	Activity 12 - Celebrate You
Page 24	More by Dara Publishing and Strictly Essential Clothing

Copyright © 2017 Dara Wisdom and Empowerment Coaching / Reea Rodney

If You're HAPPY and You Know It CLAP Your Hands

Improving Your Self-Celebration
Introduction

It is very easy to feel comfortable with ourselves when our accomplishments are acknowledged by a peer, family, or when we get the grades we were hoping for. But what happens if we don't meet our own expectations or the expectations of others? Or, what if something unexpected happens? Often, these unforeseen circumstances can throw us off; we may begin questioning our self-worth and doubting our abilities.

This workbook series was designed as a guide to provide children with the proper tool needed to enhance, improve and develop positive self-esteem traits and practices. Children are introduced to a self-esteem and self-evaluation activities which are created to help them recognize their strength and weakness and provide the foundation for them to build on.

About the Coach / Author
Reea Rodney

Reea Rodney is a wife and mother of three wonderful children who resides in Brooklyn, New York. Originally from Trinidad & Tobago, a small twin island located in the West Indies, she migrated to the United States in 2006 in pursuit of a better life for her family. In addition, Reea is also an Empowerment Life Coach, Children's Author, Motivational Speaker, a Childcare Provider and a Medical Assistant.

Because of her innate passion and desire to help children, Reea was inspired to write children's books via her publishing company, Dara Publishing LLC. She wanted to assist not only the children who were under her care, but children all over the world. Fueled by this purpose, Reea became a Certified Life Coach. The result? Dara Wisdom and Empowerment Coaching. In addition, Reea aspires to be a positive voice of empowerment for children that she herself lacked when she was a child.

She seeks to educate parents and young children through her dynamic mini workshops and self-improvement workbooks. Topics such as Self-Esteem, Self-Love, Self-Celebration, Self-Confidence and Bullying are topics that Reea addresses through her programs. While most of these life skills are not taught in schools they are valuable to a child's overall wellbeing and development.

If You Are HAPPY and You Know It CLAP Your HANDS
Improving Your Self-Celebration
What is Self-Celebration?

Have you ever scored in a game or completed a task you've been working on, like a puzzle or an art project, and at the end you did a little dance as you smiled?
Yes! You know the one… that dance where you point your fingers in the air as you shake your tushy and make a silly face. Well that's an example of what Self-Celebration is.

Have you ever done self-celebration when you accomplished something? If the answer is yes, write what you did and how it made you feel.

_____

_____

_____

_____

_____

If You Are HAPPY and You Know It CLAP Your HANDS

Improving Your Self-Celebration
Why is Self-Celebration Important?

Self-Celebration acts as a fuel that motivates us to always do our best, even in the areas where we are weak. Self-Celebration also lightens up the mood when you are engaged in serious tasks, like learning how to ride your bike, or learning math.

Each accomplishment, big or small, should be recognized and celebrated by you. Self-Celebration helps you to be motivated. With high motivation, you will enjoy yourself more in every area of your life. People who are highly motivated usually attain more.

Self-Celebration is simply rewarding yourself. Doing so will have a positive impact as you will feel more motivated to build more positive habits.

Now that you've learned why Self-Celebration is important, can you think of five (5) reasons why you should practice Self-Celebration?

1 _____

2 _____

3 _____

4 _____

5 _____

If You Are HAPPY and You Know It CLAP Your Hands
Improving Your Self-Celebration
Why Celebrating your Failure is Important?

As previously stated, Self-Celebration is praising yourself for who you are and things that you have accomplished. It's also celebrating your failures. Yes, Failures! I know you may be thinking 'why on earth would I want to celebrate if I failed at something?'

The idea is that once you've experienced that sad and low feeling that's comes with failure, but is still willing to try again, you're much more likely to have the passion, experience, and the lessons to succeed the next time you try. Self-Celebrating when you fail should motivate you to try again.

Have you ever failed at something and celebrated your efforts and hard work? If the answer is yes, write what you did and how it made you feel.

If You Are HAPPY and You Know It CLAP Your HANDS

Improving Your Self-Celebration
Positive Impact of Self-Celebration

Self-Celebration can have a wealth of positive impact on you and the people who spend time with you. Your mom, dad, brother, sister and even your friends at school would benefit. You may be wondering why is that?

Well, Self-Celebration promotes Self-Confidence, Self-Esteem and Self-Love which overall makes you a very highly motivated person and fun to be around.

Here are a few positive impacts Self-Celebration can have on you:

- Build on successes – feel a sense of achievement everyday;
- Recognition for what you've accomplished;
- Have more fun while doing a task;
- Makes you happy and fulfilled;
- Build self-confidence;
- Motivate others.

Can you think of five (5) positive impacts of Self-Celebration?

1. _____
2. _____
3. _____
4. _____
5. _____

If You Are HAPPY and You Know It CLAP Your HANDS
Improving Your Self-Celebration
Fun Ways to Promote Self-Celebration at Home or School

Here are a few fun ways to promote Self-Celebration at home or at school:

- Put a coin in a jar every time you feel good. When the jar fills up, treat yourself to something nice. You will feel even better!
- Break into a chicken dance, or your very own signature dance to celebrate a happy moment or accomplishment.
- Pat yourself on the back when you answer a question correctly in class.
- Shout at the top of your voice "I did it!" when you completed a task. Sing aloud, no matter how bad you think you sound.
- Jump, higher and higher until you can't get yourself up anymore.

Can you think of five (5) ways you can practice Self-Celebration in School and at Home?

1. _____
2. _____
3. _____
4. _____
5. _____

If You Are HAPPY and You Know It CLAP Your HANDS
Improving Your Self-Celebration
Parents Tips for Promoting Self-Celebration?

Share the Importance about Self-Celebration: It is a great way to teach your young child about celebrating themselves.

Have your own Personal Self-Celebration Routine: It will give your child a visual outlook as children mimic what they see.

Emcouragement: Encourage your child to celebrate their victories.

Celebrate Moments: Help your child identify moments in their lives that are worth celebrating such as: graduating preschool, not being scared at their dentist visit, or even making a new friend at school or the park.

Chores at Home: Assign them a household chore and compliment them when they've completed their task.

Break it into Down: Help them accomplish a task that is difficult for them by breaking it into steps and celebrate each step as they work on it. For example, when teaching them how to tie their shoelace, first teach them how to untie the shoelace, then loose the lace, followed by making the first tie, etc. and allowing them to celebrate each moment.

Make a List: Make a list with them of things they must do or things that are worth celebrating. As they do it, celebrate it with them. For example:

- Completing their homework without a fuss;
- Going to bed on time and staying in bed;
- Working on their listening skills;
- Playing nicely with friends;
- Being a good helper around the home or school;
- Showing kindness to family and friends;
- Trying something new.

Copyright © 2017 Dara Wisdom and Empowerment Coaching / Reea Rodney

Activity 1
Introduce Yourself

Keep in touch with how you are feeling on a daily basis.

Introduce Yourself:

Draw a picture of you.

Your Name: _____

My Birthday

Month: _____

Day: _____

I am _____ years old.

My Favorites!

Color: _____

Sport: _____

Song: _____

Holiday: _____

Animal: _____

TV Show: _____

Food: _____

I'm Happiest When:

I'm Am Most Proud Of:

Activity 2
It's All about Me

Let's celebrate all the things you love about yourself. For example, I love my hair because it's so long and shiny. You can write on it or draw/paint on the things you love about yourself.

Activity 3
Celebrating Achievements

Make a weekly task list with Mom and Dad of things you would like to do at home or at school. It can be putting the dishes in the sink after you are done eating, or not coming out of your bed during the night, or being a good listener. Once you have completed the task, make a big deal about it and celebrate the moment.

	Week 1	Week 2	Week 3	Week 4
Monday	Task	Task	Task	Task
Tuesday	Task	Task	Task	Task
Wednesday	Task	Task	Task	Task
Thursday	Task	Task	Task	Task
Friday	Task	Task	Task	Task
Saturday	Task	Task	Task	Task
Sunday	Task	Task	Task	Task

Activity 4
Things I Like About Myself

Give yourself some praise by listing five (5) things you love about yourself and CELEBRATE.

 **Things I Like About Myself**

1. _____
2. _____
3. _____
4. _____
5. _____

Activity 5
Faceing Your Fears

Disappointments and failures are a part of life; therefore, it is important to learn to celebrate your efforts even if you fail the first time. Make a list of the things you are afraid of doing because you feel you are not good enough and why you are afraid. For example, I'm afraid to learn how to roller-skate because I'm scared of falling and humiliating myself.

Overcome Your Fear Worksheet

Things I'm afraid to do and why:	The date I faced my fear:	How I felt after facing it and what the outcome was?

Now go and do all the things you've listed that you are afraid of and celebrate yourself by doing a victory dance or something special. Once you OVERCOME YOUR FEARS you will build your Self-Esteem as you would immediately become a winner. It's also important to know that it's okay to fail, or make mistakes. It's part of learning!

Activity 6
Praise Yourself

Giving yourself a compliment. This should be very easy to do, but for most it may be very difficult. Learning how to compliment yourself and your efforts is a very important factor in learning how to celebrate yourself, accomplishments, and failures.

Let's be honest... You rock. There's a lot about you to praise. Building your confidence means recognizing what you are great at. List at least five (5) things that you can praise yourself about. If you are struggling with this, try to ask yourself, "What would a friend say about me?"

1. _____

2. _____

3. _____

4. _____

5. _____

Activity 7
My Gratitude List

A huge part of being able to celebrate yourself is being able to love yourself for who you are - inside and outside.

Directions: In each heart, write something positive about yourself. Color and decorate your tree.

Activity 8
I Am As...

Let's celebrate all the things that make you who you are.

Quick as a ▭

Funny as a ▭

Smart as a ▭

Sweet as a ▭

Happy as a ▭

Silly as a ▭

Loud as a ▭

Brave as a ▭

Strong as a ▭

Tall as a ▭

Copyright © 2017 Dara Wisdom and Empowerment Coaching / Reea Rodney

Activity 9
Reward Certificate

Let's celebrate your accomplishments with this reward certificate. List five (5) things that you have worked hard at improving.

Activity 10
Celebrating the Little Things

Over the next month, each day list something you have done at home or at school that you believe is worth celebrating.

Ex. Something you have learned - New game

Something you have done - help an old lady crossed the street

Something you have shared – a pencil

Celebrating The Little Things.
A Month of Gratitude

#		#	
1		16	
2		17	
3		18	
4		19	
5		20	
6		21	
7		22	
8		23	
9		24	
10		25	
11		26	
12		27	
13		28	
14		29	
15		30	

Activity 11
Celebrating a Hero

A hero is someone we think of as special because of the good or brave things that they have done. List why you are a hero in the activity below and why you are celebrating yourself.

Name: _____   **Date:** _____

Explain what makes you a hero by listing some of the brave and kind things you have done.

Activity 12
Celebrate You

What about you that make others smile?
In this activity write a letter to yourself and list three (3) reasons why you make others smile.

Dear _____

Thinking of you makes me happy
Because of these three reasons:

1. _____

2. _____

3. _____

I hope you have a happy day!

Want more great reading?
Check out these books in our series!

Juniper and Rose

"Check out our Dara Publishing Store at
www.darapublishingstore.co
for our children's books, clothing, and much more.."

Strictly Essentials Styles by DARA

Visit our website for more: https:www.darapublishing.co/strictly-essentials/

Dara Wisdom and Empowerment Coaching